Patriarchal Lineage of the Shultz Family

By: Horace Michael Shultz Jr.

The Shultz family name has changed with time and is evidently subject to change further with time. All names held herein are reflective of the name that is inscribed on the headstone of the person (if such a stone can be found). The Shultz name is properly spelled "Schultz" but few use the somewhat silent "c" so it arrived as "Shultz". It appears that upon arriving in the U.S. (or the colonies that later became the U.S.) the "z" was swapped for an "s" in an effort to Anglicanize the name, so as to fit in with the fostering American culture more easily. However, in some cases, no reasonable explanation can be concluded. For example, Alexander Preston Shultz (son of Martin "S.E.") had a daughter die at the age of 20 in 1880. He and his wife buried her in Jefferson City with the inscription "D.V. Daughter of A.P. and E.C. SHOLTS", yet when his wife died just five years later, and he died 27 years later, they were both buried under a stone that reads "Alexander P. Schultz and his wife Elizabeth C. Schultz". This discrepancy is inexplicable, specifically when considering that Alexander would have overseen the inscription on his daughter's stone referring to his wife as "E.C. Sholts" and then five years later overseen his wife's own stone being inscribed with "Elizabeth C. Schultz". Alexander was a Sergeant in the Civil War, so he was likely a literate man. He would have known the difference, and yet approved of both in such a short time span. There is no clear and rational explanation.

Nevertheless, this account is not a true genealogical study. This is a lineage account leading from the most recent generation back as far as possible in the patriarchal line.

1. Heinrich Christoff Shultz (January 31, 1680/84 – May 15, 1736) [52 yrs]

To the current date (July 7, 2017), Heinrich is the progenerator of the Shultz family

name. Heinrich was born in Darmstadt, a city in the state of Hesse, Germany. There is very little

known about him other than that he had a son named Johan Velten (Valentine) and a wife named

Sophe (Sophia) Margaretta (Margarette). However, the attached document is a baptismal

certificate for his son Velten (in which Heinrich is named as father) that is placed in the city of

Prößdorf, Lucka, Germany - nearly 4 hours away from Darmstadt by today's travel, or a 3 day

walk. This would evidence that they either lived elsewhere during the boy's childhood, or lived

elsewhere entirely. There have been some claims made that Heinrich was the son of a couple by

the names of Christov and Maria Shultz. They are said to have both been born in 1662 and lived

in Bundesrepublik, Germany, about a 30-minute drive or a one day walk from Darmstadt.

Nevertheless, these claims are unsubstantiated and have absolutely no proof behind them, and

thus are treated as mere rumor. The very location of Bundesrepublik is questionable. It is

important to remember in all of this that the nations and places named are often the common day

terms used. Germany, as a single nation, was not existent until 1871. Before that, it was a

confederation of nation-states, the most powerful of which was Prussia. The majority of events in

this lineage would have been technically on Prussian land. Bundesrepublik is a common term for

the entire Western half of Germany after the Berlin Wall was erected, so this casts further doubt

on the theory of Christov and Maria being earlier ancestors, given their total lack of

documentable existence, birth and death dates, and place of origin.

2. Johan Velten (Valentine) Shults (July 24, 1715 – Nov. 16, 1745) [30 yrs]

Johan Velten Shults was born in Darmstadt, Hessen, Germany to his father Heinrich Christoff and mother Sophe Margaretta. He was baptized into the Lutheran Church on October 29th of his birthyear. On September 10, 1731, he (16 years old) and his assumed wife Elizabeth (18 years old) traveled to Rotterdam, Holland to board a ship called "The Pennsilvania Merchant." The ship stopped in Dover, England, before making its trek across the Atlantic, finally landing in Philadelphia, Pennsylvania. Upon arrival, Velten and Elizabeth traveled to the frontier on the west side of the Susquehanna River in Lancaster County, Pennsylvania. Today, this is in York County, Pennsylvania. Sadly, Elizabeth died giving birth to Velten's first son Henrich Henry in 1735. On October 16, 1735, just four months after Elizabeth died, Velten remarried a woman named Maria Stocker and moved to the Conestoga Township in Lancaster County, Pennsylvania. They were married at their home church, Christ Lutheran Church, in the town of York, Pennsylvania. Velten is recorded as having been a key contributor to buying the church a blank book. Maria's family had arrived from Switzerland on a ship named "Charming Betty" just two years after Velten had arrived. Maria and Velten had five children before his passing in 1745 in York, Pennsylvania. To date, his burial site is unknown. There is a Johan Shultz interned at the Hebron Moravian Cemetery in Lebanon, PA, some 25 miles from Lancaster and 50 mi. from York. However, the birth and death dates are incompatible.

It is important to note, when Velten and Elizabeth sailed from Holland, they were not the only "Shultz" couple on the ship. Another man, Hans Martin Shultz, and his family were on the ship over. Nevertheless, no kinship can be established between these two "Shultz" families, based on both the differentiations in their spelling of "Shultz/Shults" and the age gap (Hans Martin was 51 when Velten was 16).

3. Johan Martin Shultz MD (Apr. 3, 1740 – Nov. 1787) [47 Yrs]

Johan Martin Shultz was born in the Manchester Township, Lancaster County, Pennsylvania, to his father Johan Velten and mother Maria Eva Shultz. According to the attached article laying out the history of the area in which they lived, there were no shoemakers in the region. Hence, Johan was raised as an apprentice learning the skill of shoemaking, and so practiced until his departure from the region later in life. On July 28, 1761, Johan married Julianna Stentz at Christ Lutheran Church, confirming he was still Lutheran. In 1761, he volunteered to apprentice a 16-year-old named Philip Bayer in the skill of shoemaking, vowing to release him from his apprenticeship by his 21st birthday. Just two years later, Johan petitioned the courts to release him from the vow of apprenticeship and inscribe Bayer to another local shoemaker, Daniel Peterman. Upon being granted his release, Johan (and family) moved to "Carolina". On Thursday, 24 December 1772, he bought 300 acres of land from Henry Dellinger and his wife Hannah for 10 pounds, Proclamation money. This land was located on the head waters of Leeper's Creek on Lick Run adjoining John Dellinger in Tryon County, North Carolina. By 1764, he and his family had made the journey to Mecklenburg County, North Carolina. When they arrived there, they settled in the area of Killian's Creek and Leeper's Creek, or Lick Run which is now the eastern part of Lincoln County, North Carolina. On Saturday, 21 June 1777, he and his wife sold their 300 acres of land on head waters of Leeper's Creek and Lick Run adjoining John Dellinger for 70 pounds, Proclamation Money to Nicholas Shrum and Henry Dellinger in Tryon County, North Carolina. Both he and his wife signed in the old German script. In this deed, Martin was named as 'Doctor Martin Shultz.' Apparently before 1777 he had received his training as a physician and surgeon while living in Mecklenburg and Tryon Counties, North Carolina. In November of 1779, Martin purchased 200 acres of land in

Washington County, NC (now Tennessee). Washington County was later divided into Sullivan County, TN, and all future records were kept there.

In Fall of 1780, General Cornwallis, Commander of the British Army, was in Charleston, South Carolina, planning an invasion of North Carolina and needed Major Ferguson to secure his left flank from the Appalachian Mountains. Ferguson began assembling Loyalists into a militia to secure the area. Hearing of it, the Patriots began scrambling to assemble their own militia and attack the Loyalist militia. Colonel Isaac Shelby commanded Sullivan County, North Carolina (later Tennessee) and Lieutenant-Colonel John Sevier commanded Washington County, North Carolina. With Washington County having just been divided into Washington and Sullivan Counties one year prior, and Martin owning close to 400 acres in that region, it is hard to say which Colonel he would have been under the command of, though noteworthy East Tennessee Historian Jim Shults claims that Martin was in fact under the command of John Sevier. This claim is supported by the two men's continued relationship after the war.

The Patriots rallied a force of close to 1,000 soldiers to attack the Loyalist militia at King's Mountain. On October 7, 1780, the "Over Mountain Men" (as they came to be called because of their being assembled from over the Appalachian Mountains) attacked the Loyalists and devastated their militia. The Battle of King's Mountain lasted a little less than two hours, and was an absolute victory for the Patriots. According to Pat Alderman's "Over Mountain Men", Martin Shultz was a private in this militia.

Also, on pages 261 and 262 of "The Bear-Guard of the Revolutions" by James R. Gilmore, it is found that: '...A terrible night followed the terrible day of the battle. The cold was intense, and a strong wind swept across the mountain. The wounded lay around where they had fallen, upon the bare ground, among the unburied dead, with no shelter but the grey sky above them. There were no splints for their shattered limbs, no bandages for their flowing wounds, and **only one surgeon among the entire two hundred and fifty [in Col. Sevier's regiment]**. Said one who witnessed it, 'The scene was heartrending in the extreme---the groans of the dying, and the constant cry of the wounded for 'Water!' 'Water!'" It appears that the only Patriot surgeon was in Colonel John Sevier's Company of 250 men, and it is strongly believed that this surgeon was Doctor Martin Shultz.

Furthermore, according to a statement published in the *Rivington's Royal Gazette*, New York, on February 24, 1781, Lieutenant Anthony Allaire of the British Army accounts, "We lost eighteen men killed on the spot-Capt. Ryerson and thirty-two Sergeants and privates wounded, of Maj. Ferguson's detachment. Lieutenant M'Ginnis of Allen's regiment, Skinner's brigade, killed; two Captains, four Lieutenants, three Ensigns, **one Surgeon**, and fifty-four Sergeants and privates, including the wounded, wagoners, etc. The militia killed, one hundred, including officers; wounded, ninety; taken prisoners about six hundred; our baggage all taken, of course."

It is further accounted in an official recanting of the battle under the signature of all of the Patriot Colonels, "It appears from their own provision returns for that day, found in their camp, that their whole force consisted of eleven hundred and twenty-five men, out of which they sustained the following loss:--Of the regulars, one Major, one captain, two lieutenants and fifteen privates killed, thirty-five privates wounded. Left on the ground, not able to march, two captains, four lieutenants, three ensigns, **one surgeon**, five sergeants; three corporals, one drummer and fifty-nine privates taken prisoners." With this said, it is apparent that there was an extreme shortage of trained physicians in both militias – to the point that only one is accounted of in the entire Loyalist regiment - his name was Dr. Uzal Johnson. Thus, it can be reasonably concluded that Martin Shultz was the only trained physician in the Patriot Army at the Battle of King's

Mountain, and was the only surviving surgeon after the battle's completion. Due to the repeated accounts that there were no trained physicians in early Tennessee and North Carolina, it is further extremely likely that Johan Martin Shultz was the first doctor in Tennessee's History.

After the war's completion, Martin and John Sevier maintained communication. After becoming the governor of the new region (then called "Franklin" soon to be Tennessee,) Sevier signed the Treaty of Dumplin Creek on June 10, 1785, securing an agreement with the Cherokees to allow settlements into Franklin (Tennessee), specifically near the Big Pigeon River (current day Sevier County). According to Goodspeed's "History of Tennessee", Martin and Frederick Emert (another Revolutionary War veteran) were conscribed to settle this new land. The area is now known as Emert's Cove. However, there was other land that belonged to Martin predating this period, although it was not strictly lawful until the Treaty of Dumplin Creek made it so. It is accounted on page 138/139 of "History of the Lost State of Franklin" by Samuel Cole Williams that sometime between August 19, 1779 and August 9, 1787, Stockley Donelson, the County Surveyor for Sullivan County, made a survey of a land entry on 'south side of Holston River' and noted the error in the calculation of acres in this land entry. On Thursday, 9 August 1787, Martin received the land grant from the State of North Carolina, although the entire Holston River is contained within the state of Tennessee (or Franklin as it were).

Johan Martin Shultz MD died in the Fall of 1787, just two years after officially settling into the Tennessee area (hence the settlement becoming known as "Emert's Cove"). His son Martin "SE" Shultz performed the majority of the familial duties from his passing on, specifically caring for his now widowed mother until her death in Emert's Cove in 1810.

But, to return to the situation of the early settlers—
For some time after these early settlements were made
there was neither a shoemaker nor tanner in any part of
what is now York county. A supply of shoes for family
use was annually obtained from Philadelphia; itinerant
cobblers, travelling from one farm house to another, earned
a livelihood by mending shoes. These cobblers carried
with them such a quantity of leather, as they thought
would be wanted in the district of their temporary visit.
The first settled and established shoemaker in the county,
was Samuel Landys, who had his shop somewhere on Kreutz
creek. The first, and for a long time the only tailor, was
Valentine Heyer, who made cleathes for men and women.
The first blacksmith was Peter Gardner. The first school-
master was known by no other name than that of "Der
Dicke Schulmeister."

The first dwelling houses of the earliest settlers were of
wood; and for some years no other material was used in
the construction. But about the year 1735, John and
Martin Shultz each built a stone dwelling house on Kreutz
creek and in a few years the example was numerously followed.

Of the settlements in the neighborhood of the *Pigeon
Hills*, we shall speak more particularly when we come to
that part of our history embracing the borough of Han-
over.

SETTLEMENT OF "THE BARRENS."

For several years after the settlements were made in the
neighborhood of the Pigeon Hills and on Kreutz creek,
the inhabitants of those regions were the only whites in the
county. But about the year 1734 '35 and '36, a number of
families from Ireland and Scotland settled in the south eastern part of the county, in what is now known as the "*York
Barrens*." These families consisted principally of the better order of peasantry—were a sober, industrious moral and
intelligent people—and were for the most part rigid pres-
byterians. Their manners partook of that simplicity,
kindness and hospitality which is so characteristic of the
class to which they belonged in their native countries.
The descendants of these people still retain the lands

4. Johan Martin "S.E." Shults Jr. (Dec. 27, 1772 – Nov. 11, 1846) [73]

Johan Martin Shults Jr. was born the son of Johan Martin (MD) and Julianna Shultz in Tryon, North Carolina. In 1785, after the signing of the Treaty of Dumplin Creek, the Shultz family (with 12 year old Martin) moved across the mountains into Franklin to settle what would soon become Sevier County. After his father died in 1787, Martin took over much of the familial responsibility, specifically tending for his mother (which he did until her death in 1810). This is relevant in indicating his character, because Martin was far from the oldest son. He was much closer to being the youngest child altogether.

While Martin was far too young to have fought in the Revolutionary War, and didn't live to see the Civil War, he was commissioned to serve at the rank of Captain in the Sevier County Militia. Thankfully, he was never called into combat (or at least to this point there aren't any reports thereof even though he did serve during the War of 1812). For his service, he was awarded several land grants in Tennessee (as reflected in the attached documents).

On July 28, 1792, Martin married Barbara Ann Emert, daughter of Frederick Emert, with whom his father had moved into the new territory. Within 10 months their first son (Philip) was born – the first of their 13 children.

During the period of 1796-1806, records show Martin Shultz Junior owned lands in the area of Webb's Creek by right of occupancy. He sold it to Joseph Anderson in 1808 prior to the issuance of land grants by the State of Tennessee. The records read in part as follows:

(1) 'State of Tennessee District South French Broad and Holston

'In pursuance of the law in such cases made and provided and by virtue of a Deputation from Robert Wear Esq surveyor for the district Aforesaid I have surveyed for Martin Shults 11 Acres 1 Rood 1 Chains of land held and Claimed by right of occupancy Situate in Sevier County on the waters of Webbs creek having such form and Boundaries as represented surveyed 2nd May 1807 Given under my hand this 6th day June 1807.

'Variation of the Needle 5 Degs East Laid down by a Scale 40 chs to the inch

Thomas Price, D S

'I Martin Shults for and in Consideration of the sum of Twenty five dollars to me in hand paid the Receipt whereof is hereby acknowledged do hereby assign over the within Survey of Lane unto Joseph Anderson In witness whereof I have hereunto set my hand and seal this 4th day February 1808.

Test William Freazier Marting Shults (Seal) Isaac Love

'State of Tennessee Sevier County Court February Sesions 1808

'This was the Execution of the above Transfer of land being duly proven in open Court by the oaths of William Feasher and Isaac Love the subscribing Witnesses thereto and the same is admitted to record

Test Saml Wear C S C'

(2) 'State of Tennessee District South French Broad and Holston

'In pursuance of the laws in such cases made and provided and by virtue of a Deputation from Robert Wear Esqr surveyor for the District Aforesaid I have surveyed for Martin Shults 42 Acres 2 roods 3 Chains of land held and Claimed by right of Occupancy situate in the County of Sevier on the water Webbs creek having such form and Boundaries as represented Surveyed 1st May 1807 Given under my hand this 6th day June 1807.

'Magnetic Variation 5 degs Laid down by a scale 40 chs to the inch

Thomas Price, D S

'I Martin Shults for and in Consideration of the sum of Seventy five Dollars to me in hand paid the Receipt Whereof is hereby Acknowledged do hereby Assign over the Within Survey of land to Joseph Anderson In witness whereof I have hereunto set my hand and seal this 4th day of February 1808.

Test William Freasher Marting Shutls (Seal) Isaac Love

'State of Tennessee Sevier County Court February Sessions 1808

'This was the Execution of the above transfer of Land being duly proven by the oaths of William Freasher and Isaac Love the subscribing witnesses thereto and the same is admitted to record Test Saml Wear C S C'

There is another land grant for Martin Shultz from the State of Tennessee. He entered 55 acres 1 rood 5 chains on the waters of East Fork of Little Pigeon River. It was surveyed on 29 August 1807 and granted on 9 May 1810. This land joined vacant lands and lands of Frederick Emert in the Emert's Cove area.

According to Sevier County, Tennessee Surveyors Book #1 - 5,000 Acres of land entry for William Roberts and Isaac A. Miller dated 12th day of May 1830. It reads as follows: 'State of Tennessee) 'By virtue of Entry No. 760 dated 12th Sevier County) day of May 1830 'I have surveyed for William Roberts and Isaac A. Miller as joint entrees five Thousand acres of land in said County on the waters of Birds Creek and the west fork of little Pigeon River 'Begining on a Pine at the ford of the Glade Branch near Captain Shults muster ground...Surveyed 23 day of November 1838.

D. Emmitt & C C John Mullendore, Cty Curveyor Thos. McCarter.

In 1813, Martin Shultz Junior signed a petition asking the Tennessee General Assembly for redress on the validity of land claims in Sevier County, Tennessee. This petition is in Tennessee State Library and Archives, Nashville, Tennessee.

Martin Shultz Junior entered numerous land entries in Sevier County, Tennessee during his lifetime. They include: 160 acres-5 August 1824; 15 acres-12 August 1824; 50 acres-28 August 1824; 222 acres-28 August 1829; 69 acres-28 August 1829; 31 acres-28 August 1829; 50 acres-28 February 1832; 31 acres-16 October 1836; and 113 acres-11 March 1839. Martin Shultz Junior and his wife, Barbara Ann Emert, were listed in the 1830 and 1840 Federal Census of Sevier County, Tennessee.[1] (Martin is listed under "Martin Shoults")

[1] *Source: 'Smoky Mountain Clans', Donald B. Reagan, 1978, p 6, 70. 'Smoky Mountain Clans, Volume 2', Donald B. Reagan, 1983, p 6, 16. 'Ownby-Watson Family History', Percival David Park, May 1985, p 32. Rosa Lee Downey notes, 16 June 1983, p 42. 'The Book of Ragan/Reagan', Donald B. Reagan, 1993, p 407. 'In the Shadow of the Smokies', Smoky Mountain Historical Society, 1993, p 404. 'Sevier County, Tennessee and Its Heritage', 1994, p 341.*

Martin lived out the entirety of his life in Emert's Cove (now Pittman Center) and died there on November 11, 1846. He is buried there and his stone remains to this day (photos attached).

To this point, it is unknown why he was called by the name "S.E." However, we know for certain that this was his chosen name, because it was engraved on his headstone.

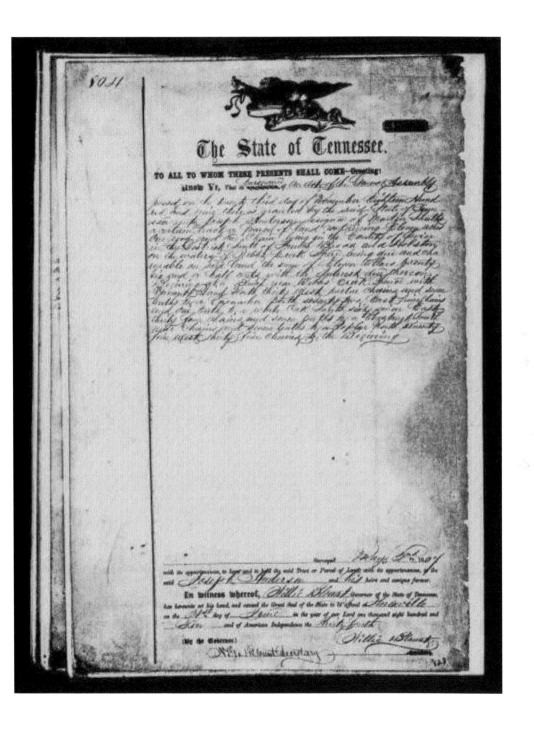

Land Grant dated June 21, 1810.

Land Grant dated August 8, 1824.

Emerts Cove Cemetery.

Grave of Martin "S.E." Shults Jr.

Photo taken June 13, 2017.

Close up of inscription on original headstone.

Reads: Martin

                  Shults = SE

                  Died Nov 11 1846

Photo taken June 13, 2017.

Grave of Barbara Ann Emert

Photo taken June 13, 2017.

Close up of Barabara Ann's original headstone

Reads: Barbara Ann Shults

                Born March 26, 1770

                Died Sept. 23, 1875

Photo taken June 13, 2017.

5. Philip S. Shultz (May 26, 1798 – Feb. 12, 1871) [72 years]

Philip S. Shultz was born the son of Martin "S.E." and Barbara Ann Shults in Sevier County, Tennessee. Philip's life is one of the more mysterious lives in the Shultz history. Philip was the firstborn son of a successful and valiant settler who had earned a name for himself and had forged a strong relationship with one of the wealthiest men in Tennessee (Frederick Emert) by marrying his daughter (Barbara). He inherited possibly the best life that any Shultz had been given regarding possibility of prosperity since the family came to the Americas four generations before him.

Philip was married three times in his life. His first marriage to Elizabeth Huskey (1820) ended in divorce sometime between 1846 and 1859 (the first divorce in the Shultz family to this point). His second wife (Minerva Amillia) died just three years after they were wed (1859-1862). Then Philip died just four years after marrying his last wife, Mary (1867-1871).

The truly interesting thing about Philip is the wealth that he amassed in his lifetime. In an Anderson County will probate hearing (No. 312, December 17, 1872), Philip S. Shults' estate was said to include "Tennessee State Grant 24671 (half interest with Frederick Emert] 21 May 1842 for 4000 acres in Sevier county bounded by Dunn's Creek and the Cocke County line", and "Tennessee State Grant 23913 [also half interest with Frederick Emert] 20 Aug 1841 for 2520 acres in Cocke County on the headwaters of Cosby Creek."

To make the rich even richer, Philip wasn't only wealthy in land or coin. At current date there are 16 "Shultz/Schultz/Shults" men who are known to have fought in the Civil War from the state of Tennessee. 11 fought for the Confederacy (South) and 5 fought for the Union (North). Of the 5 Shultz's that fought for the Union, 4 were Philip's sons, and the other was

Philip's brother, Alexander Preston. Alexander was granted 5,000 acres of land bounded by the East Prong of the Pigeon River, Webb's Creek, the Cocke/Sevier County line, and a line well up on the slope of the Western escarpment of the Smoky Mountains. This means that between these two brothers, they owned over 11,000 acres of East Tennessee land from mountains to rivers and everything between, and were the only Shultz's rewarded for their service in the Civil War.

Yet, what makes Philip's life interesting is not his wealth, it is the evident loss of all of it. When Philip died in 1871, his estate was auctioned off, and anything that his wife or children wanted to keep had to be purchased. He left no inheritance to his decorated sons, nor any land for them to make a life on. It appears that Philip either squandered his entire fortune, or was the victim of one of the worst robberies to have ever been accomplished. There is a record of Philip having been a founding member, and partial owner, of the "Sevier County Silver, Copper, Lead, and Zinc Company." It was incorporated in 1867, just four years before his death (documentation attached). What impact this had on his finances is currently unknown.

Philip was buried in "Black Cemetery" in Anderson County, Tennessee, where he had moved after the death of his second wife. In what seems like a fitting misfortune to occur even beyond the grave given the knowledge of his life, the cemetery in which Philip was interred was purchased by the TVA in 1962 and relocated to accommodate a steam plant. His coffin was excavated (along with his wife, Mary's) and relocated to a new location nearly 200 yards away. Attached below are photos of the cemetery, the stone, and recent photos showing the new location. In order to find the grave, one must walk nearly 150 yards through the woods to find the cemetery, and then the stone can be seen standing, despite a small tree growing through the plot.

Henry McCall, Isaac R. Hawkins, B. F. Harrison, John Bell, Adam Hall, Young W. Allen, —— McGill, Alvin Hawkins, A. D. Bennett, and John Norman, and their associates, successors and assigns, be, and they are hereby constituted, a body corporate and politic, by the name and style of the "Huntingdon Manufacturing Company;" and by that name and style shall have succession for fifty years; shall have power to contract and be contracted with, sue and be sued; to make and use a common seal; to purchase and hold real estate, receive donations in land, or other property, or money; to erect buildings, put up engines, machinery, and other fixtures, for the purpose of manufacturing cotton, wool, furniture, iron, plows, and machinery of various kinds.

Huntingdon Manuf'ng Company. / **Powers.**

SEC. 25. *Be it further enacted,* That the capital stock of said company shall be twenty thousand dollars, divided into shares of fifty dollars each. Said company shall have power to increase the capital stock of said company to two hundred and fifty thousand dollars. **Capital Stock.**

SEC. 26. *Be it further enacted,* That when the sum of ten thousand dollars of stock shall be subscribed, said stockholders may, after giving ten days' notice of the time and place of meeting, assemble and elect five of their number Directors of said company, who shall hold their office for twelve months, and until their successors are elected and qualified. Said Directors shall elect one of their number President. They shall also elect such other officers as they may deem necessary for the carrying on of the business of said company. Said company, when organized, shall have power to make such by-laws, rules and regulations, as they may deem necessary for the successful carrying on the business of said company, not inconsistent with the laws of this State. **Election of Directors, etc.** / **Duties.**

SEC. 27. *Be it further enacted,* That said company shall have all the rights, benefits and privileges, granted to other corporations, and be subject to such general laws as may be passed, from time to time, for the government of corporations; *Provided,* that no State aid shall be granted said corporation. **Rights and Powers.**

SEC. 28. *Be it further enacted,* That Perry M. Shults, Pleasant W. Shults, Philip S. Shults, Wilson Duggan, P. L. Duggan, and Robert C. Duggan, and their associates, successors and assigns, be, and they are hereby, constituted a body corporate, by the name and style of the "Sevier County Silver, Copper, Lead and Zinc Company;" and by that name shall have succession for ninety-nine years, and shall be competent to sue and be **Sevier Co'nty Silver, etc., Company.**

sued in any Court of law and equity; to have and to use a common seal, to alter the same at pleasure; to establish, ordain and change, any by-laws that may be necessary for the government of the company, which by-laws shall not be inconsistent with the Constitution of the United States, and the Constitution and laws of the State of Tennessee; to purchase, hold and dispose of such real estate, leases, mines, minerals, silver, copper, lead and zinc, and personal property, as they may desire, or be necessary for the legitimate transaction of their business; to mine, dig, bore, forge, roll, smelt, transport, work, manufacture, refine, and vend the same; issue such number of shares of the stock of said company, at the respective par value thereof, as may be determined and agreed on by said company, and to have the right to pay of stock of the corporation for such mining interest; to construct roads from their mines to a navigable river or railroad, now constructed or to be constructed; and to make connections and turn-outs for their purposes, etc.; that the capital stock of said company be five hundred thousand dollars, to be divided into such shares as the company may determine, which may be increased or diminished, as the company may determine. The President and Directors, when elected, shall regulate the proportion of stock, which may be issued to each member, on application; the company to have, enjoy and exercise, all rights and privileges belonging and incident to corporations, except the right to issue notes, or engage in the business of Banking. **Powers, Privileges, etc.** / **Same.** / **Capital stock.**

SEC. 29. *Be it further enacted,* That the right to alter, change, amend, or repeal this charter, is reserved to any subsequent Legislature. **Reserved.**

SEC. 30. *Be it further enacted,* That Jno. S. Van Gilder, F. A. R. Scott and W. B. Rogers, their associates and successors, be, and they are hereby, incorporated, a body politic and corporate, under the name and style of the "Knoxville Leather Company," and in that name may own and hold so much real and personal property as may be necessary for the use and purposes of the corporation. **Knoxville Leather Co.**

SEC. 31. *Be it further enacted,* That said company may have a capital stock, not to exceed one hundred thousand dollars, divided into shares of one hundred dollars; may have such number of Directors, officers, clerks, agents, &c., as they may desire, and elect them for such time as they may choose. **Capital Stock.** / **Officers.**

SEC. 32. *Be it further enacted,* That said company

shall have all necessary and proper powers incident to the manufacture of leather goods, and leather, and such other articles as they may desire to manufacture; and full power to make such by-laws as they may find necessary for their government. **Powers.**

SEC. 33. *Be it further enacted,* That this Act shall take effect from and after its passage.

J. S. MULLOY,
Speaker pro tem. of the House of Representatives.
JOSHUA B. FRIERSON,
Speaker of the Senate.

Passed March 11, 1867.

Black Cemetery place marker.

Photo taken June 13, 2017.

Site of the original Black Cemetery.

Photo taken June 13, 2017.

Philip's Head and Footstone in the relocated Black Cemetery

Photo taken June 13, 2017.

Close up of Philip's Headstone. Reads:

       P.S. Shultz

       BORN May 26, 1798

       DIED Feb. 12, 1871

Photo taken June 13, 2017.

6. Eli H Shults (Jan. 6, 1822 – June 22, 1869) [47 Yrs]

Eli H Shults was born to his father Philip S. and Elizabeth Huskey Shultz in Jones Cove, Sevier County, TN. The first record that can be found for Eli after moving out on his own is the U.S. census from 1850, in which it is recorded that he lived in Eastern Subdivision 12 of Sevier County, Tennessee. This subdivision is found to the Southeast of Sevierville, with Veteran's Blvd as its western border, Highway 321 as its southern border, and Pittman Center Road as its eastern border. This new residency was roughly 15 miles West of his birthplace in Jones Cove, and roughly 20 miles Northwest of Emert's Cove.

Eli married Mary Polly Large in 1854. Eli and Mary had 5 children between 1856 and 1867, and according to the attached census' from 1870 and 1880, none of their children attended school. Mary was also incapable of writing, so it is unlikely that she would have been able to teach her children anything at home. For this reason, it is safely assumed that all five of the Shults children were illiterate into adulthood at least.

Eli enlisted in the Union Army on September 16, 1862 in Sevierville, Tennessee, committing to a 3 year term in the Tennessee 2nd Cavalry, E Company. His enlistment document is attached, and describes his physical characteristics as such: "Age – 32. Height – 5'7". Complexion – Fair. Eyes – Blue. Hair – Black. Born – Severe Cty. Occupation – Farmer."

Eli fought and achieved the rank of Corporal by the end of the war. One noteworthy conflict that he engaged in was the Battle of Mossy Creek in what is now Jefferson City, Tennessee, on December 29, 1863. The Tennessee Encyclopedia of History and Culture describes the details of the battle as such:

"The Confederate army began to bend back the flanks of the Union position while the center, anchored by Captain Eli Lilly's artillery battery, held back the rebel onslaught. At about 2 p.m., Lilly's battery, low on ammunition and receiving accurate musket fire, retired to another hill behind A. P. Campbell's brigade. At this point, a Southern victory seemed assured. As the Confederates under Brig. Gen. Frank Armstrong attempted to roll up the Federal line from north to south, Campbell ordered one of his cavalry regiments to attack Armstrong's men. The Federals charged headlong into the southern line, wreaking havoc and stopping the Confederate advance. Over on the Union right, Colonel LaGrange's men entered the fight after a hasty summons had brought them back from Dandridge. The cavalry charge and arrival of Federal reinforcements convinced General Martin that the time for retreat had come, and he made an orderly withdrawal to his position held before the start of battle. His army was also low on ammunition. During the evening, the Confederate army fell back to Morristown. The Federals held their position at Mossy Creek, having inflicted possibly four hundred casualties on the Confederate side compared to over a hundred of their own."

According to John Andes and Will Mcteer in their book "Loyal Mountain Troopers: The Second and Third Tennessee Volunteer Cavalry in the Civil War" it was the Tennessee 2nd Cavalry that charged on the confederates, securing the flank "wreaking havoc and stopping the Confederate advance." Eli H. Shults (and his uncle Alexander Preston) was in that cavalry.

However, we know for certain that it was not only the Tennessee 2nd Cavalry that charged. In May of 2017, Horace Michael Shultz Jr. was conscripted by Dr. David Needs of Carson Newman University to renovated "Branner Cemetery", the burial site of many of the fallen soldiers at the Battle of Mossy Creek. One of the soldiers interred there was Capt. E.J. Cannon of the Tennessee 1st Cavalry. He died during the charge previously described. Michael Shultz restored his stone, along with several others. Regardless of the mixing of the units at this disorganized skirmish, history will remember the Tennessee 1st and 2nd Cavalry for holding off the Confederates at the Battle of Mossy Creek, and by all indications, the Shultz family can claim that Eli Shults was an integral part of that victory.

Eli returned home from war and had two children with his wife before dying in 1869. He was buried in Spurgeon Cemetery, in Dunn Creek, Sevier County, Tennessee. His wife and family were given pension for his military service after his death. Photos of his headstone and the pension information are attached.

| 2 Cav. | Tenn. |

Eli H. Shults

_____, Co. _E_, _2_ Reg't Tennessee Cav.

Appears on

Company Descriptive Book

of the organization named above.

DESCRIPTION.

Age _32_ years; height _5_ feet _7_ inches.

Complexion _Fair_

Eyes _Blue_; hair _Black_

Where born _Revere Co. Tenn._

Occupation _Farmer_

ENLISTMENT.

When _Sept 16_, 186_2_

Where _Revereville Tenn._

By whom _Lt Col D M Ley_; term _3_ y'rs.

Eli Shults enlistment document with physical description.

S | **2 Cav.** | **Tenn.**

Eli H. Shults

Corpl., Co. *E*, 2 Reg't Tennessee Cavalry.

Age *32* years.

Appears on **Co. Muster-out Roll,** dated

Nashville Tenn., *July 6*, 186 *5*.

Muster-out to date *July 6*, 186 *5*.

Last paid to *June 30*, 186 *5*.

Clothing account:

Last settled *Sept 16* 186 *3*; drawn since $ 100

Due soldier $ .... 100; due U. S. $ 100

Am't for cloth'g in kind or money adv'd $ *6.3* 50/100

Due U. S. for arms, equipments, &c., $ 100

Bounty paid $ .... 100; due $ *100* 00/100

Eli Shults payment for military service. Reflects rank as Corporal

S | 2ᵈ Cav. Tenn

Eli. H. Snylts

Corp. , Co. C , 2 Reg't Tenn Cav

Appears on

Hospital Muster Roll

of   No. 11 U. S. A. General Hospital,

at   Nashville, Tenn.,

for _Mar. & Apr._, 186 4

Attached to hospital:

When ___Feb. 27___, 1864.

How employed _____

Last paid by Maj. _Fullerton_

Report for Muster Roll for March and April 1864.

Present on Feb. 27, 1864. Reflects rank as Corporal.

NAMES.	RANK.	AGE	ENLISTED.	MUSTERED.	REMARKS.
Nicodemus, Mart H		21	Sep 1 63	Jan 26 63	Died Nov 3 62
Russell, Riley		23	"		Died March 19 63
Russell, Morgan		31	"	"	Killed in action at Sugar Crk, Dec 26 64
Redwine, Elkanoh F		22	"	"	Died Feb 16 63
Sartin, William		18	"	"	Died Feb 1 63
Urwin, George W		19	"	"	Died April 7 64
Vinyard, Samuel A	Privates.	21	"	"	Died Feb 20 63
Wilbourn, William		28	"	"	Died Dec 6 62
Walker, Joseph		28	"	"	Died Mar 17 65 of wds rec bef Nashville, Dec 16 64
Bira, John		30	"	"	Died Feb 20 63
Homer, William B		19	"	"	Deserted Jan 2 63
Marine, David		24	"	"	Deserted Oct 25 63
Northern, Alford A		24	"	"	Deserted Jan 5 63
Northern, Francis M		28	"	"	" "
Ghinas, James		22	"	"	Deserted Jan 2 63
Walker, Newton		24	"	"	" 24 65

COMPANY E.

NAMES.	RANK.	AGE	ENLISTED.	MUSTERED.	REMARKS.
Daniel B Duncan	1 Lt	30		Sept 16 62	
Sanders McMahan	2d Lt.	27		"	
William Benson	1 Ser.	35			1 Sergt from enrollment
Joel W Hicks	Sergt.	30			Sergt from enrollment
Richard R Reagan	"	32			" "
Alexander P Shults	"	46			" "
Joseph P Waters	"	22			" "
William Lax	"	25			" "
Jonathan Hicks	"	28			Ap Sergt fr privt Mar 1 65
Morris Norris	Corp.	25			Pris of war since Oct 12 63
John Large	"	32			
James Webb	"	39			Corp since date of last paymnt: jd by trans fr Co K Mar 1 63
Albert H Parton	"	25			Corp since date of last paymnt
Eli H Shults	"	32			" " "
William R McGaha	"	22			" " "
Jesse A Giles	"	24			" " "
David Shoemaker	Bksm	22	September 16, 1862	January 26, 1863	Blksm since date of last paymnt
William A Cerson	Sadl'r	28			Saddler " "
John W Shults	Wgnr	21			Wagoner " "
Bryant, James J	Privt.	17			
Duggan, Archibald M	"	39			
Gregory, John	"	22			
Gunter John	"	18			
Giles, John M	"	29			
Hicks, David	"	28			
Hicks, John	"	34			
Henry, William	"	41			
Henry, George	"	20			
Hearst, Vincent	"	26			
Johnson, James C	"	26			
Johnson, William C	"	28			
Jenkins, Stauberg	"	19			
Kener, Thomas J	"	24			
Murrell, Nathaniel	"	26			
McMahan, Henders'n	"	22			
McMahan, James	"	30			
McGaha, John	"	26			
Norris, Isaac	"	20			
Ogle, Noah	"	29			
Proffitt, David	"	17			

Tennessee 2ⁿᵈ Cavalry Roll

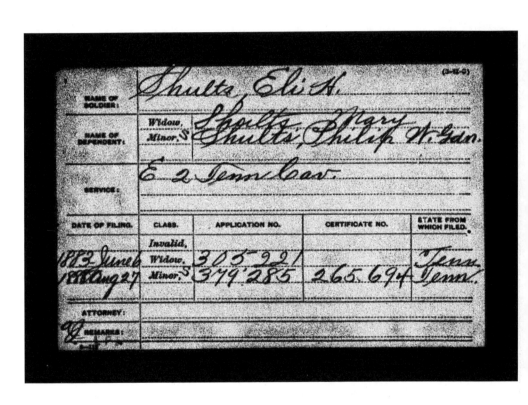

Pension application from Mary Shults and Philip W. Shults.

Spurgeon Cemetery, Dunn Creek, Sevierville, Tennessee.

Headstone of Eli Shults.

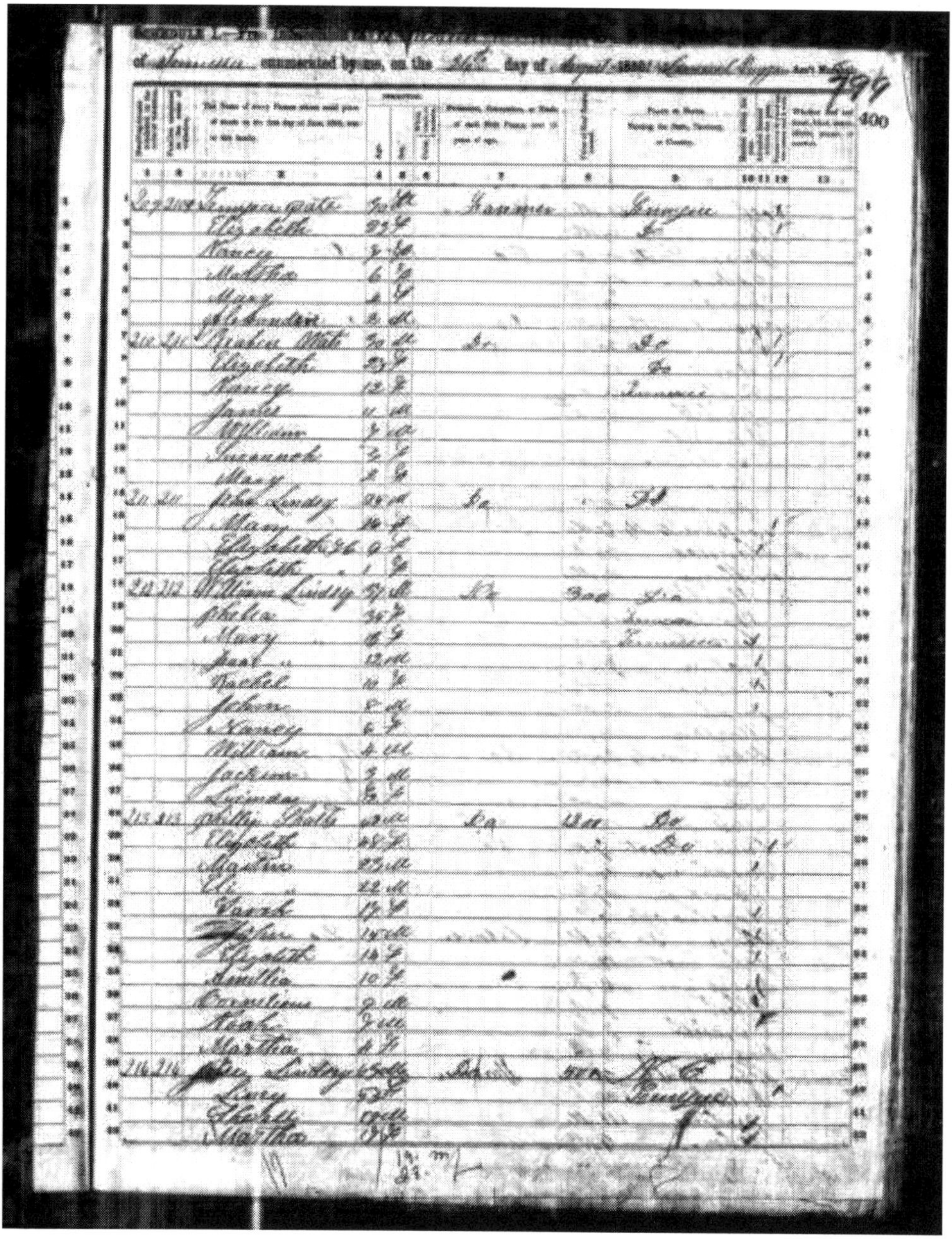

Eli H appearing on the census of his father Philip S in 1850.

Schedule 1.—Inhabitants in District No 2, in the County of Sevier, State of Tennessee, enumerated by me on the 26 day of July, 1870.

Post Office: Sevierville

E. M. Vance, Ass't Marshal.

347

1	2	3	4	5	6	7	8	9	10	11	12	13	14	15	16	17	18	19	20	
1		Fox Nicholas	18	M	W	Farm laborer			Tennessee	1						/				1
2		Margarett	15	F	W	Without Occupation			Tennessee	1										2
3		Thomas	6	M	W				Tennessee	1										3
4		Martha B	4	F	W				Tennessee											4
5	79 79	Shults Noah	25	M	W	Farm labor		387	Tennessee									/		5
6		Rebecca J	25	F	W	Keeping house			Tennessee											6
7		Milla	30	F	W	Domestic servt			Tennessee											7
8	80 80	Klumper Archibald	54	M	W	Farm laborer		120	Tennessee									/		8
9		Jane	32	F	W	Keeping house			North Carolina					/						9
10		Margarett C	12	F	W	At Home			North Carolina					/ /						10
11		William	9	M	W				Tennessee											11
12		Archibald	6	M	W				Tennessee											12
13		John G	4	M	W				Tennessee											13
14		Samuel	2	M	W				Tennessee											14
15		Buddy	6/12	M	W				Tennessee		26									15
16	81 81	Shivers Wilene	18	F	W	Keeping house			Tennessee					/ /						16
17		Sarah J	3	F	W				Tennessee											17
18	82 82	Shults John S	34	M	W	Farmer	1000		Tennessee							/				18
19		Harriett	30	F	W	Keeping house			Tennessee					/						19
20		Newton B	13	M	W	At Home			Tennessee					/						20
21		Martha A	11	F	W	At Home			Tennessee					/						21
22		David W	9	M	W				Tennessee											22
23		Eliza A	4	F	W				Tennessee											23
24		Graham G	2	M	W				Tennessee											24
25	83 83	Shults Mary	37	F	W	Keeping house	600	157	Tennessee											25
26		Ellen	13	F	W	At Home			Tennessee					/						26
27		Phillip W	11	M	W	At Home			Tennessee											27
28		Alexander M	9	M	W				Tennessee											28
29		Mary	8	F	W				Tennessee											29
30		Lenora	3	F	W				Tennessee											30
31	84 84	Rienhart John W	42	M	W	Farm labor		400	Tennessee									/		31
32		Sarah E	37	F	W	Keeping house			Tennessee											32
33		Ann E	11	F	W	At Home			Tennessee					/						33
34		William W	3	M	W				Tennessee											34
35		Ulisus G	1	M	W				Tennessee											35
36	85 85	Crosby William	35	M	W	Farm labor		172	Tennessee					/ /				/		36
37		Mary	30	F	W	Keeping house			Tennessee											37
38		John	12	M	W	At Home			Tennessee					/ /						38
39		Thomas	10	M	W	At Home			Tennessee					/ /						39
40		Laura	6	F	W				Tennessee											40

No. of dwellings, 7   No. of white females, 19   No. of males, foreign born, 00   No. of insane, 00

" families, 7   " colored males, 00   " females, " 00

" white males, 21   " females, 00   " blind, 00

Mary Shults accounting for the family after Eli's Death. 1870.

7. Philip W. Shultz (January 1, 1859 – March 8, 1935) [76 Yrs]

Philip W. Shultz was born to his father Eli H. and mother Mary Polly Shultz in Sevierville, Tennessee. From census records, we know that Philip lived with his widowed mother through his teen years and would have likely been expected to take up the familial responsibilities on the farm, being the only male in the household.

Philip married Rachel McMahan in Sevierville, Tennessee, on April 8, 1880, at the age of 21. It is likely that they lived nearby to his mother until her passing on August 3, 1886. After this point, records show his residency being in District 17 of Sevierville, Tennessee (as of 1910). District 17 now includes the current cities of Jefferson City and Sevierville, along with the towns of Dandridge, New Market, and White Pine.

Little else can be said of Philip W. To his credit, he was given little to start with, so his humble life is reflective of only his humble beginnings. Philip died of stomach cancer on March 8, 1935. (Death certificate attached). His wife applied for Social Security in 1936 after his passing.

He was buried in Webb's Creek Cemetery, Sevier County, Tennessee. A photo is attached of the cemetery but at this date no photo of his individual headstone exists.

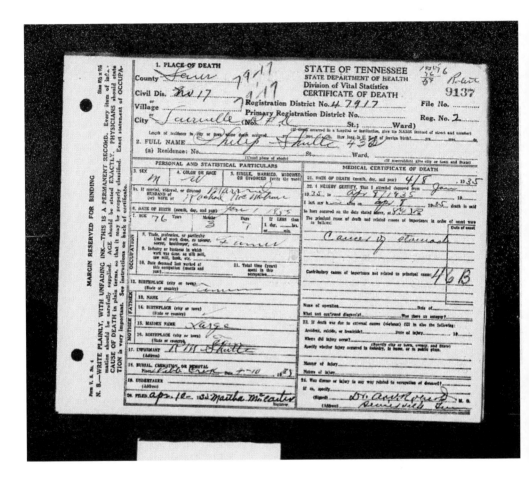

Death certificate of Philip W. Shultz

Webbs Creek Cemetery, Sevierville, Tennessee.

8. Rockford Clinton Shultz (March 20, 1881 – Nov. 20, 1965) [84]

Rockford Clinton Shultz was born to his father Philip W. and mother Rachel McMahan Shultz in Sevier County, Tennessee. Born into a farming family, he learned the craft and made it his life's work. Farming evidently served him fairly well because as early as the 1920 census it is recorded that he owned his own home.

The interesting aspect of Rockford's life is his marital status.

By most family traditions the belief is that Rockford's first wife was Carrie Marinda McCarter (Known as "Rindy"), and that they got married around 1919. This would be supported by the 1920 census (attached) in which he is listed: "Shults, Rockford C. Head of Household. Married. Aged 39." Beneath him is: "Shults, Carrie M. Wife. Married. Aged 22." There are no children listed on the census, so it seems that this was the beginning of Rockford's family. "Rindy" Shultz was the mother of Rockford Clinton "R.C." Shultz Jr in 1928.

However, the 1900 census (attached) records the following: "Shults, Rockford. Head of Household. Born May, 1881. Age – 19. Married. *Number of Years married:* 1. Farmer." Below him: "Alice. Wife. Born Mar. 1879. Age – 21. Married. *Number of Years married:* 1. *Mother of how many children:* 1. *How many children living:* 1." Below her: "Roy V. Son. Born Feb. 1900. Age – 3/12 (3 months)." Thus, we know that Rockford was in a relationship with a woman and they had a child when he was 18 (Roy Victor "Vic" was born a month before Rockford's 19th birthday). Family records have their marriage date at April 23, 1899 (some sources say April 20th). While this early marriage is uncommon in 21st Century America, this would not have been uncommon in 1899. However, the shocking detail is that according to Cocke County marital records (marriage license attached) Rockford married Mary Alice Branam on October 25, 1909. This may explain why little is known about Mary Alice. In late 19th and early 20th Century America, having a child out of wedlock would have been disgraceful, so the story was likely hidden from further generations.

For certain, by 1920, Rockford was married to Carrie Marinda "Rindy/Rinda". It is further explanation for why "Vic" does not appear on this census under the household of Rockford and Marinda – he would have been 20 years old at the time and likely no longer living at home. Some doubt has been cast by family members claiming that the marriage certificate was not for the right Rockford Shultz because it was issued in Cocke County while the vast majority of Shultz's lived in Sevier County. However, a draft registration card (attached along with Rockford's personal draft registration card) filled out by Vic on Sep. 12,1918, lists Rockford as his father and Rockford's home as "Cosby, Cocke County, Tennessee." This verifies both the relation, and the residency of Rockford.

Still yet, there is one name that appears on the 1930 census that is mysterious. The census reads: "Shultz (note that the name is spelled with a 'z' for the first time) Rockford. Head of household. Age – 49. Married. *Age at first marriage: 18.*" Beneath him: "Lurenda. Wife. Age – 34. Married. *Age at first marriage: 16.*" Below her: "Clay B. Son. Age – 8." Below him: "Roy C. Son. Age – 2." It would be easiest to explain this mysterious "Lurenda" away as a typo, given that the only appearance of this name is in this census, and that no one knows anything else about her. Still, it is hard to believe that they would get the name incorrect for someone that appeared on the previous census by first and middle name, as well as getting the age wrong. 10 years prior Marinda was listed as 22 years old, and at the time of the census Lurenda was listed as 34. The age would have been provided either by a birth year, or just a testimony – either way, if "Lurenda" is "Marinda", she would have had to have gotten her own age or birth date wrong. The issue remains to be solved of how long Rockford and Marinda had been married. It would have had to be 18 years (Meaning she would have married Rockford in 1912), as her first marriage was at the age of 16. This brings forth one of three possibilities of how this could play out:

1] Rockford divorced Mary Alice just three years after becoming legally married to her. Their son, Vic, would have been 9 years old when his parents got legally married, and only 12 years old when his parents divorced. This would not have been well received in 20th Century America.

2] If family tradition holds true that Carrie Marinda married Rockford around 1919, then the complication of divorcing a woman with a small child is done away with because Vic would have been 19 years old. However, the new issue is that Carrie Marinda would have had to have been married previously because of her account of having been married first at the age of 16, despite being 22 in 1919 when she would have married Rockford. So, in the event that Rockford did not divorce Mary Alice while Vic was a child, the unfortunate truth arises that Marinda was divorced also.

3] There was a 4th woman named Lurenda that Rockford married that was hidden from family traditions.

In any case, on the 1940 census (attached) Rockford is yet again married to another woman, Nannie. To be fair, Rindy/Rinda died in 1935, so this new marriage is easily understandable. Nannie is the woman that the majority of the descendants (still living in 2017) remember as Rockford's wife.

Rockford died on November 20, 1965. He is buried in Shady Grove Cemetery in Tellico Plains, Tennessee. To his right lies Rindy Shultz and to his left lies Nannie Shultz, though at current date her stone stands in need of repair.

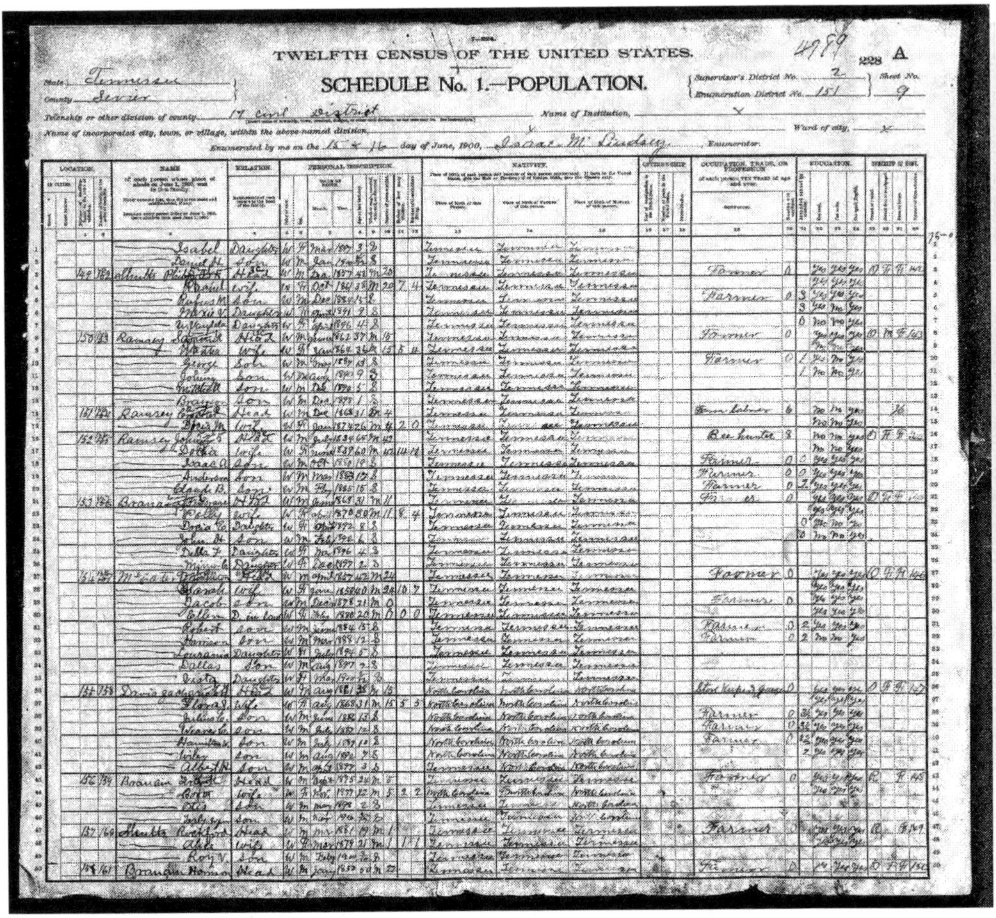

Census from 1900: Rockford, Alice, Roy V.

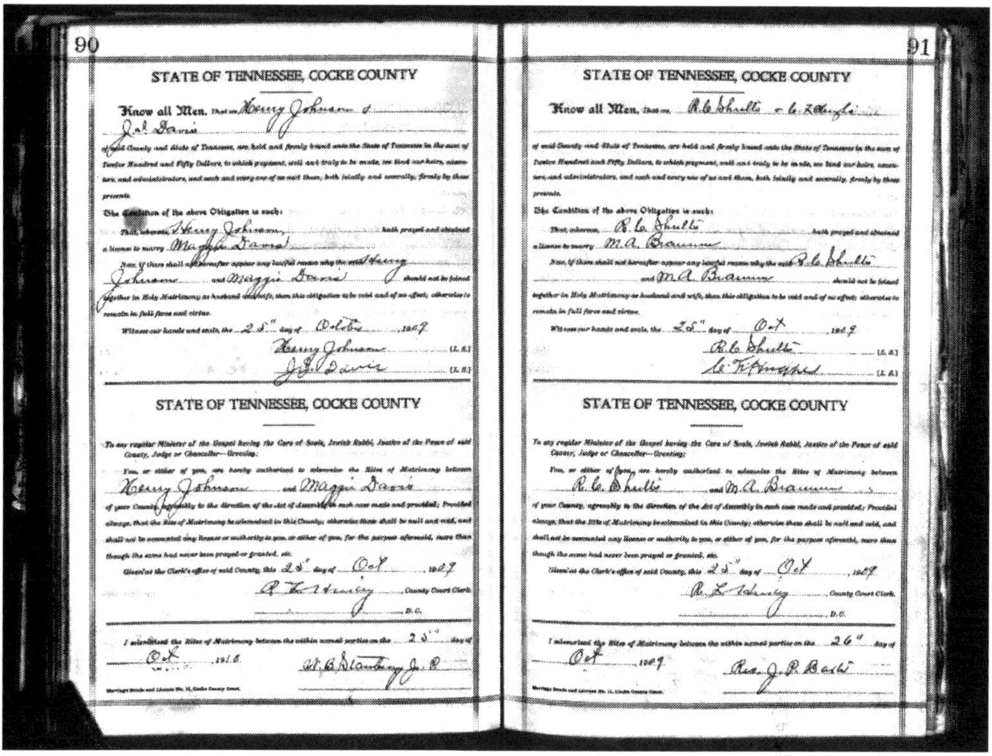

90

STATE OF TENNESSEE, COCKE COUNTY

Know all Men, that we Henry Johnson & J. L. Davis

The Condition of the above Obligation is such:

That, whereas, Henry Johnson hath prayed and obtained a license to marry Maggie Davis

Witness our hands and seals, the 25th day of October 1909

Henry Johnson [L. S.]

J. L. Davis [L. S.]

STATE OF TENNESSEE, COCKE COUNTY

Henry Johnson and Maggie Davis

Given at the Clerk's office of said County, this 25th day of Oct 1909

County Court Clerk.

D.C.

Oct 1909

91

STATE OF TENNESSEE, COCKE COUNTY

Know all Men, that we R. C. Shults & C. L. Hughes

The Condition of the above Obligation is such:

That, whereas, R. C. Shults hath prayed and obtained a license to marry M. A. Branam

Witness our hands and seals, the 25th day of Oct 1909

R. C. Shults [L. S.]

C. L. Hughes [L. S.]

STATE OF TENNESSEE, COCKE COUNTY

R. C. Shults and M. A. Branam

Given at the Clerk's office of said County, this 25th day of Oct 1909

County Court Clerk.

D.C.

I solemnized the Rites of Matrimony between the within named parties on the 26th day of Oct 1909

Rev. J. P. Bash

Marriage license of "R.C. Shults and M.A. Branam.

Oct. 25, 1909."

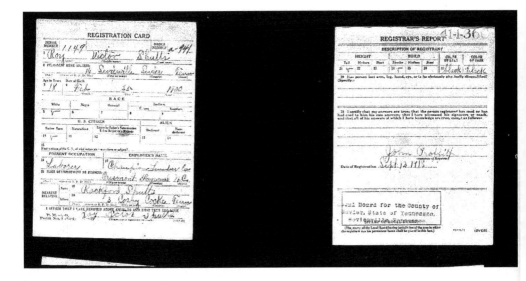

Roy Victor Shultz's draft registration card.

Rockford Shultz listed: Cosby, Cocke County, Tenn.

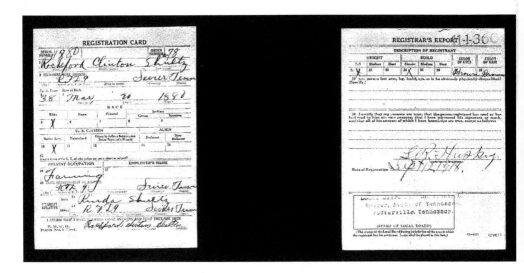

Rockford Clinton Shultz draft registration card.

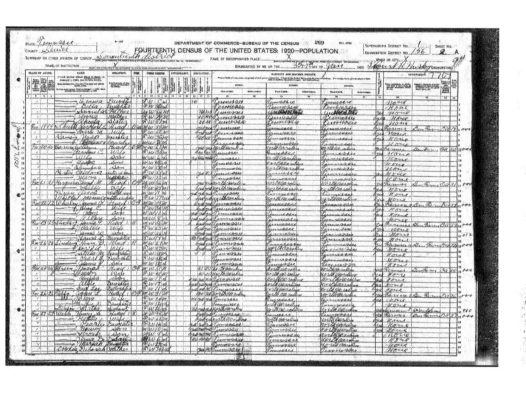

1920 Census – Rockford and Carrie.

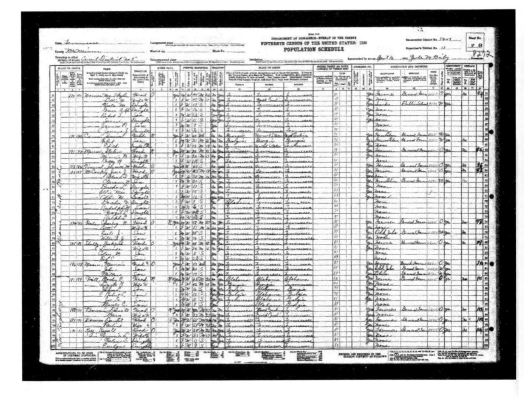

Census 1930 – Rockford, Lurenda, Clay B., Roy C.

Map of Home	**District 5, Mcminn, Tennessee**
Street Address	**Mouse Creek Road**
Dwelling Number	**185**
Family Number	**187**
Home Owned or Rented	**Owned**
Radio Set	**No**
Lives on Farm	**Yes**
Age at First Marriage	**18**
Attended School	**No**
Able to Read and Write	**Yes**
Father's Birthplace	**Tennessee**
Mother's Birthplace	**Tennessee**
Able to Speak English	**Yes**
Occupation	**Farmer**
Industry	**General Farm**
Class of Worker	**Working on own account**
Employment	**Yes**
Household Members	

Name	Age
Rockford Shultz	49
Lurenda Shultz	34
Clay B Shultz	8
Roy C Shultz	2

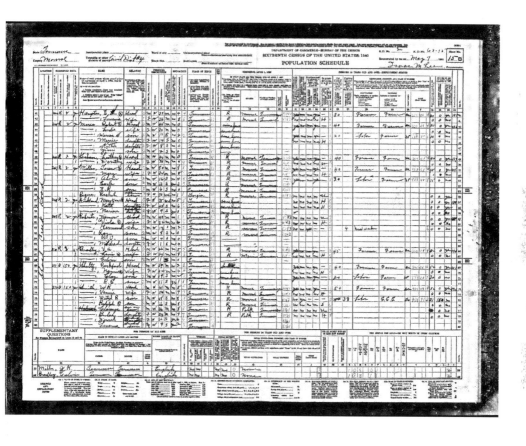

Census 1940 – Rockford, Nannie, Clay, R.C.

Rockford and Rindy's Headstone

Nannie Shultz's Headstone

9. Rockford "R.C." Clinton Shultz Jr. (Apr. 8, 1928 – 13, Jan. 2016) [87 Yrs]

Rockford "R.C." Clinton Shultz Jr. was born to his father Rockford Clinton Sr. and mother Carried Marinda, near Athens, Tennessee. According to the 1940 census (attached) he was the first member of his family to receive any form of education. By his own testimony, he got to "about 5th or 6th grade" before leaving school to begin work.

R.C. was curious about family history and affairs. He taught his children that the Shultz family had gone through a split at some point in previous generations because two brothers had gotten in a quarrel, and consequently one brother started spelling his name differently by putting a 'c' in 'Schultz'. It could be that that someone else in the family had relayed this to him as a child as well.

R.C. married Edna McKelvey on July 18, 1953. According to their marriage license (attached) R.C. was currently living in Englewood and Edna was living in Vonore. When they married, they moved onto a piece of property that Edna's family owned, now located at 128 Watt Road, Vonore, Tennessee. It was on this plot of land that they raised all of their 5 children.

R.C. made a living by working at a furniture production factory where he worked specifically in framing. He would cut the lumber and make the inner wooden frames for couches and reclining chairs. For extra money, he spent his spare time buying dead car batteries and recharging them to resell, repairing local people's lawnmowers, even changing car tires for people that didn't know how to. It appears that R.C. became an all-around handyman. He continued his father's trade of farming for the entirety of his life, and raised his children to work the garden with him every day.

There were few luxuries in the Shultz household but there were some nonetheless. R.C. and Edna bought the first automobile to have ever been owned in this line. Being a larger family, they purchased a 1960's model stationwagon – the perfect family car for their time. They also purchased the first television in this line. It was a black and white t.v. that got three channels "if the wind wasn't blowing. If the wind blew, the antennae would fall over outside and you had to go fix it." They had the first telephone installed in their house, again, the first in this line. It was a "party line" roll dial phone.

R.C. was a large man, standing around 6'2" tall, and was stout. While most Shultz men are tall and thin (refer back to Rockford and Vic's draft registration cards), R.C. was a stalky man, well put together. He could regularly be found wearing jeans and a T-shirt, though after Edna's passing in 1999, he was commonly found wearing denim overalls.

R.C. married a woman named Opal Duckett in 2000 and was married to her until her passing in 2013. They lived on Shoal Creek Road in Tellico, Tennessee. In their time together, R.C. spent most of his days tinkering with small machines, gardening, and buying and selling firearms.

R.C. died on January 13, 2016 surrounded by his family. He was laid to rest beside his wife, long awaiting, Edna McKelvey, in Mount Zion Baptist Church Cemetery, Vonore, Tennessee. The photo of their headstone is attached.

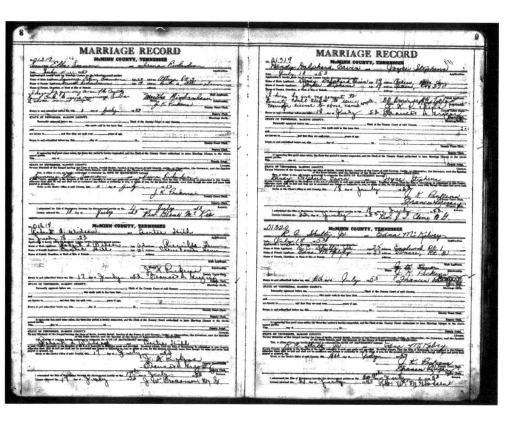

R.C. and Edna's Marriage Certification

R.C. and Edna's Headstone in Mt. Zion Baptist Cemetery

10.   Horace Michael Shultz (August 30, 1964 –

All quotes held herein are from an interview with Horace Shultz on July 12, 2017.

Horace Michael Shultz was born to his father Rockford "R.C." Clinton and Edna Lee Shultz in Vonore, Tennessee. He was named after the doctor that delivered him, Horace Michael McGuire. When Horace was a child he was taught as a boy how to garden and work on small machines such as lawnmowers and eventually large machines like cars and motorcycles.

For leisure-time he spent most of his spare days in the woods on the family property. Whether it was hunting small game with his "bb gun" or swimming in the lake that is hidden back in the woods, all of his fun time was found in nature as a small boy. From his own testimony, he and his brothers would hunt squirrels and rabbits with their dogs and if they were too tired to do that they enjoyed honing their marksmanship skills by attempting to try to shoot the wings off of dragonflies with their bb guns. Long before the time of cellphones, the boys were all expected to stay within "hollering distance" of the house. "If you didn't eat when dinner was on the table, you didn't eat." When they got bigger, R.C. would bring home parts and pieces and eventually assembled bicycles for them one piece at a time. Horace says that he learned how to ride a bike by standing on one of the pedals and pushing it down before hopping over to the other one because he wasn't big enough to reach both pedals at the same time from the seat. A big moment in Horace's childhood was when his family drove to Madisonville in the family car, and his father bought three brand new bicycles at Western Auto. "Buying three brand new bikes at one time, that was big. We even got to ride them home!" And of course, there were not gears. "We only had one-speed. The selection of bikes you could buy were either 'boy' or 'girl'. That's all we had." Horace and his brothers later spent days riding their bikes from Vonore to Loudon picking up glass Coke bottles to recycle for two cents each. Once you had ten cents, you could go to Charlie Hall's store and get an RC Cola and a Moonpie. You could even write half-cent I-O-U's (I owe you) for bubblegum at Hall's. "That was a good day. That was all before TVA bought up the land. It used to all be farmland. Now, most of the backroads that we would ride to collect the bottles are underwater from the new dams. All of the factories and plants that are there on Sweetwater-Vonore Road, like Sea Ray, that was all farmland. (*Do you remember when all of this was?*) That was in the early '70s, late '60s."

Occasionally, R.C. would take Horace into the Mount Vernon area and show him caves in which they kept milk and potatoes when R.C. was a child. Before the time of refrigerators, it was a huge find to discover an unused cave near your home in the mountains. The cold air in the cave was perfect for preserving milk and cheese, while the darkness kept the potatoes from sprouting eyes. As a special treat, R.C. and Edna would buy a pint of ice-cream for the family, and all seven of them would split it evenly.

While there were leisurely moments, childhood was burdensome in many ways. Horace and his brothers would come home from school on most days to work the garden with their father. While the luxuries listed above for R.C. were available for his children, there were many things that were not available to them. The family did not have an indoor bathroom until 1980. Up to that point they used an outhouse (and newspaper). In order to bathe (which the whole family did every Sunday) they had to carry water out to a cattle trough, fill it, and then proceed to all bathe in the same water. This was the same process for doing laundry. They had a washboard with which their mother and sister washed everything by hand every Wednesday. This sort of schedule was customary at the Shultz house. Every Friday they got to have sandwiches. On Saturday they would have hamburgers ("that was a big deal to have hamburgers") that they cooked on a woodstove, and on Wednesday they did laundry. Lacking alarm clocks, the rule was "You go to bed with the chickens. You get up with the chickens." So the whole family went to bed when it got dark, and got up as soon as the Sun came up, if not a little before.

Regarding education, Horace and his brothers and sister all went to school through the high school level. As a child, Horace didn't show much interest in school. The best thing about school when he was young was that it meant it was time for new shoes. All of the boys would get a new pair of shoes every year for back-to-school time. Most of Horace's clothes were plaid shirts and blue jeans "that we got at stores like the dollar store… only the dollar store didn't exist at that point." The boys went to school at Fork Creek Elementary School from 1st through 8th Grades (Kindergarten did not exist at this time either). Interestingly, this school had its grades placed together in two's. First and Second graders would be in class together learning basic subjects like Math and English. Once they reached 9th Grade, they went to Vonore High School. At this point, Horace said he started doing better in school because he started liking Math.

Unfortunately, from the age of 12 Horace was made to go to work. In high-school he worked on William Spence's farm on Hiwassee Knob doing various tasks such as busting wood, building and placing fenceposts, and putting up square bales of hay in the summer. "I got to go to school 2 days a week, and had to go to work 3 days a week. We all used to laugh about it because the sledgehammer and wedge were bigger than me." Two weeks into his senior year (at the age of 17), Horace quit going to school permanently, and started working full time cutting down trees to make paperwood.

Sometime between being 18 and 19, Horace moved with a friend to Okeechobee, Florida, to work on a dairy farm. In exchange for his services milking and tending the cows, he was furnished a living space and a reasonable wage. After "8 months to a year" Horace purchased a motorcycle and decided to come back to Tennessee to pick up his brother Glen and take him back to Florida with him. When he was preparing to leave, he caught a Coral Snake in his house. Knowing that they are one of the most lethally venomous snakes in the U.S., Horace put the snake into a Coke bottle and strapped the bottle across the top of his motorcycle. After leaving, he came to a full-service fueling station that pumped the customer's gas for them. However, upon seeing the live Coral Snake, the station attendant refused to fuel his motorcycle. Once Horace got back to Tennessee, he gave the snake to Bobby Wolf (a local game warden) and it was taken to the Knoxville Zoo. Some days later, Horace and Glen started making their way back down to Florida, but got caught in a thunderstorm in Chattanooga. They decided to come back to Vonore because of the storm, and subsequently never made the trip back to Florida. He moved back in with his family for a year or so, and by the age of 21 had moved out on his own to Lenoir City, Tennessee. To date, Horace has lived the remainder of his life in Tennessee.

After spending his 20's working in Lenoir City as an auto-mechanic, Horace met Susan Renea Lawhon in 1992 at the age of 28. He was working at Jack's Auto Parts (and had been for almost 10 years) across the street from a gas station/deli that Susan worked at. The story (as told from their perspectives) was that Horace would come across the street every day to get lunch from the deli because of the pretty woman working inside. Over time, Susan started noticing how muscular Horace was while working on the cars, and eventually they decided to go out. After moving in together, Horace started working with Susan's brother, Steve, building houses. They did that together for a few years. In February of 1995, they married.

Horace began working for another family friend of Susan's, Robert Gaston. Robert taught Horace how to install carpet and vinyl. He worked for Robert for 5 or 6 years before starting his own business, S&S Carpet and Vinyl. He would professionally install and perform maintenance for 17 years. He enjoyed selling and installing carpet because "Carpet sells itself. I didn't have to." Horace wasn't a salesman, and never claimed to be. He said that the worst job he ever had in his life was a door-to-door salesman, and he only did it for one day. He had followed up on a newspaper ad, and went door to door trying to sell products in Crossville. He quit after that day.

In 1997, Horace and his family moved to Sweetwater, TN. Horace coached his son, Michael, and daughter, Chelsea, in softball and basketball for their upbringings. Eventually, Horace and Susan served as commissioners of the Sweetwater little league sports organization. The peak of his coaching career was when his team "The Lady Terminators" won the State Championship for travel softball teams in Tennessee. His daughter, Chelsea, played for the team and his wife, Susan, also served as a coach.

Even into his adult life, Horace was a talented cyclist. In the early 2000's, his son Michael accounts that Horace could ride a bicycle while seated backwards. He could also ride a bicycle in 6 inches of snow. He is an avid animal lover of all types. Physically, Horace is a tall man (standing 6'0 even) and was extraordinarily toned for someone who never formally exercised. All of his physical strength was naturally had. By his own testimony, in his time as a mechanic he could lift a transmission into a car from underneath it, by himself. As a carpet installer, he would regularly carry 300 lb rolls of carpet in and out of homes by himself.

Made in United States
Orlando, FL
30 August 2022

21759994R00035